Gross Stuff at Home

by Julie Murray

Dash!
LEVELED READERS
An Imprint of Abdo Zoom • abdobooks.com

Level 1 – Beginning
Short and simple sentences with familiar words or patterns for children who are beginning to understand how letters and sounds go together.

Level 2 – Emerging
Longer words and sentences with more complex language patterns for readers who are practicing common words and letter sounds.

Level 3 – Transitional
More developed language and vocabulary for readers who are becoming more independent.

abdobooks.com

Published by Abdo Zoom, a division of ABDO, PO Box 398166, Minneapolis, Minnesota 55439.

Printed in the United States of America, North Mankato, Minnesota.
052025
092025

Photo Credits: Adobe, Getty Images, Shutterstock
Production Contributors: Jennie Forsberg, Grace Hansen, John Hansen
Design Contributors: Candice Keimig, Neil Klinepier

Library of Congress Control Number: 2024947662

Publisher's Cataloging in Publication Data

Names: Murray, Julie, author.
Title: Gross stuff at home / by Julie Murray
Description: Minneapolis, Minnesota : Abdo Zoom, 2026 | Series: Gross stuff! | Includes online resources and index.
Identifiers: ISBN 9781098288624 (lib. bdg.) | ISBN 9781098289324 (ebook) | ISBN 9781098289676 (Read-to-me ebook)
Subjects: LCSH: Cleanliness--Juvenile literature. | Home--Juvenile literature. | Housing and health--Juvenile literature. | Household ecology--Juvenile literature. | Sanitation--Juvenile literature. | Curiosities and wonders--Juvenile literature.
Classification: DDC 500--dc23

Table of Contents

Gross Stuff at Home

Home is the place people live. It provides comfort and safety. But there can be gross things living and hiding all around!

6

Dust mites live in every home. They are tiny **arachnids**. They can only be seen under a microscope. Dust mites feed on dead skin that humans and animals shed. Yuck!

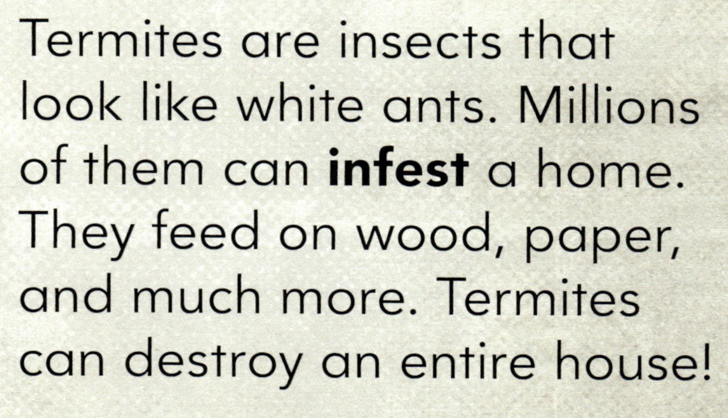

Termites are insects that look like white ants. Millions of them can **infest** a home. They feed on wood, paper, and much more. Termites can destroy an entire house!

In the Kitchen

The kitchen is a great place for germs to live and grow. Kitchen sinks, countertops, and dish sponges all hold **bacteria** that you can't see. Wiping a countertop with a dirty sponge can spread bacteria everywhere!

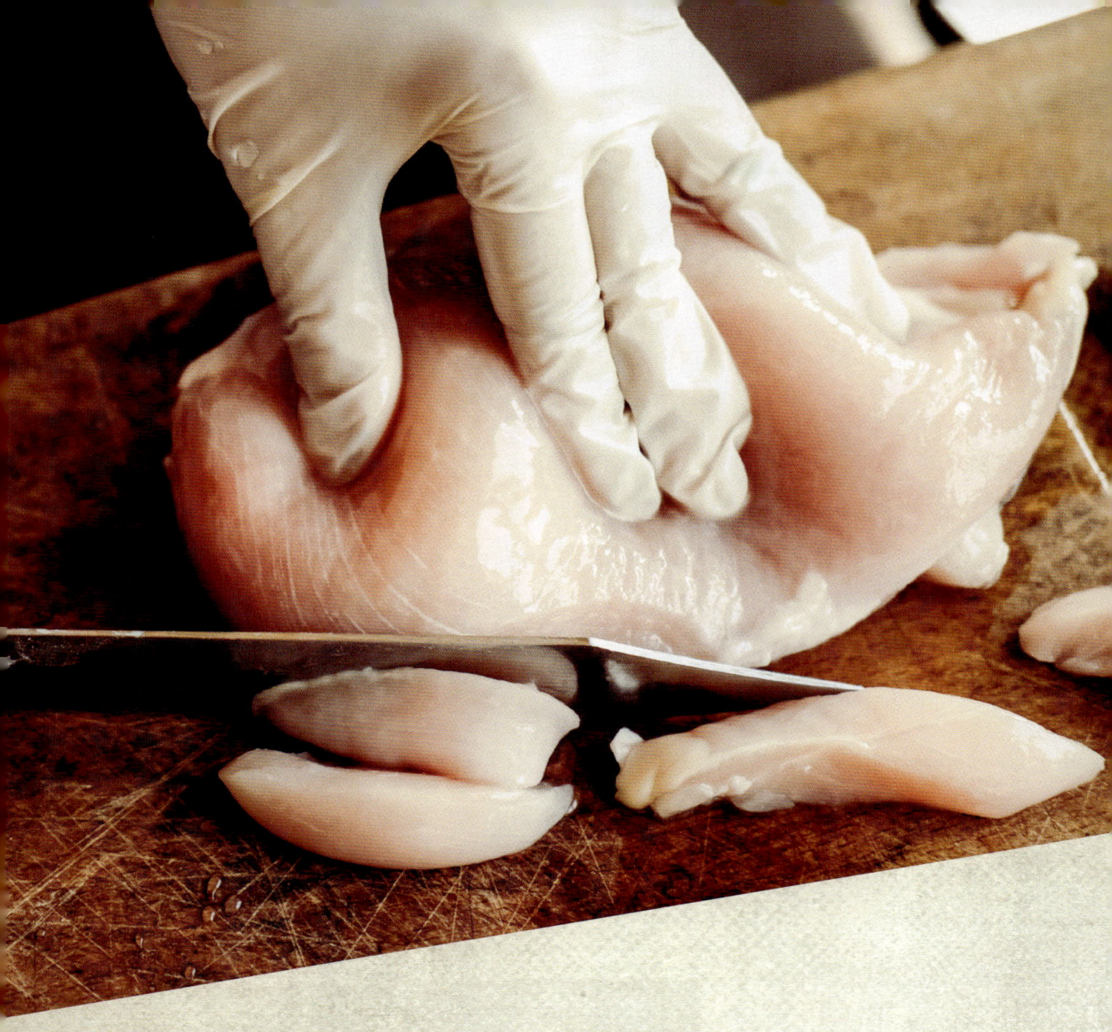

Raw meat can contain **bacteria** such as salmonella and E. coli. They cause serious illnesses. Raw meat can spread these bacteria to cutting boards, countertops, and other objects around the kitchen.

E. coli

Mold **spores** float in the air. They can land on damp food such as bread, fruit, and vegetables. Mold makes a substance that breaks down food. It takes in the food's **nutrients** and grows!

In the Bathroom

The bathroom can be the grossest room in a home. Human waste goes in the toilet. A toilet can contain millions of **bacteria** per square inch. People can close the lid when flushing to help stop bacteria from escaping.

There is a lot of **moisture** in bathrooms. Steam from showers and wet towels create damp surroundings. Mold and mildew can thrive.

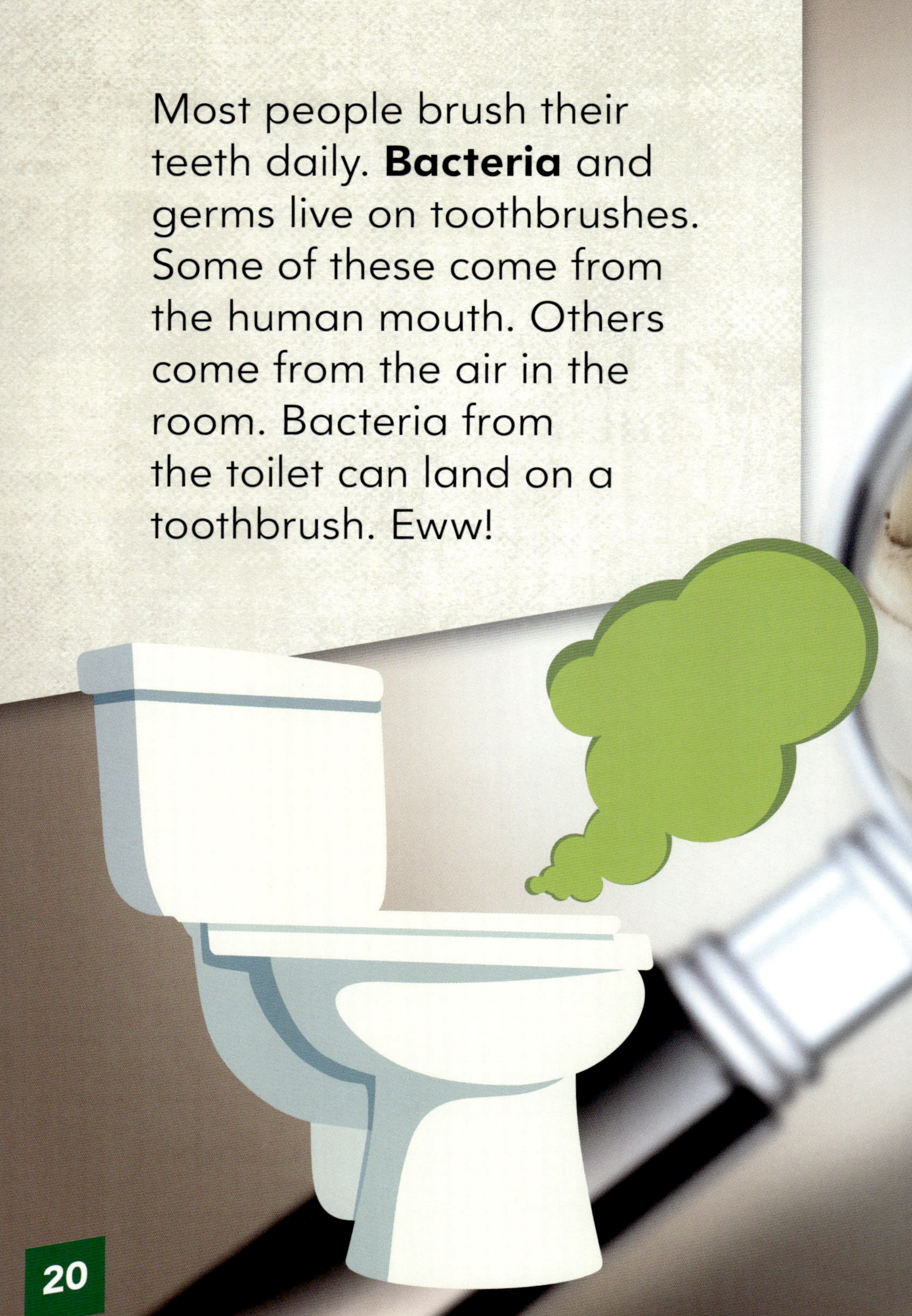

Most people brush their teeth daily. **Bacteria** and germs live on toothbrushes. Some of these come from the human mouth. Others come from the air in the room. Bacteria from the toilet can land on a toothbrush. Eww!

More Facts

- Pipes in a home can become blocked with hair and bathroom waste. They can back up and run over into sinks, showers, and toilets.
- Bed bugs hide in beds, furniture, and carpets. They feed on human blood! They bite people while they are sleeping. Bed bugs leave red, itchy marks on ankles and legs.
- Basements can hold **moisture**. They are the perfect place for mold and mildew to grow. These things can cause **allergies** and illnesses.

Glossary

allergy – a condition in which a person's body has an unusual reaction to certain things.

arachnid – an arthropod having four pairs of legs and belonging to the class that includes scorpions, ticks, and spiders.

bacteria – very small organisms that can cause disease.

infest – to spread in or overrun.

moisture – a small amount of liquid in the air or on a surface.

nutrients – things that help humans, animals, and plants live and grow.

spore – a tiny reproductive body made up of one or more cells, produced by certain animals and plants.

Index

Online Resources

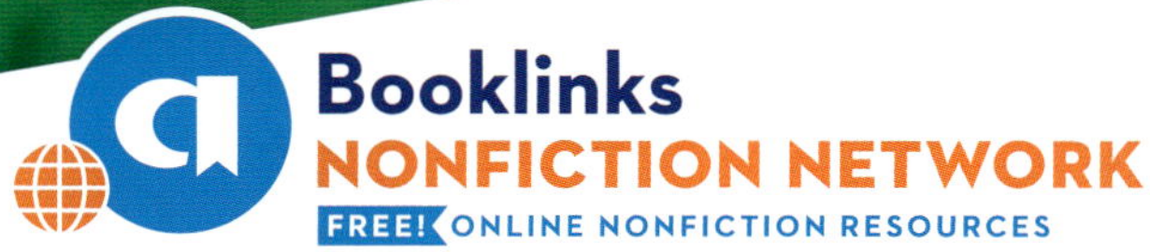

To learn more about gross stuff at home, please visit **abdobooklinks.com** or scan this QR code. These links are routinely monitored and updated to provide the most current information available.